AF492913

Contents

Introduction 4

Potty Training 6

Childcare 7

At what age can your baby start child care 8

What are your child care options for an infant 8

Choosing the best child care for your baby 19

Where can you find a caregiver? 21

Choosing a Babysitter 22

Breastfeeding Your Toddler 25

When you're ready to wean a toddler 31

Tips on Starting Potty Training 32

How will I know my toddler is ready to be potty trained .. 32

How old should my toddler be when I start potty training?
.... 33

Tips on preparing your toddler for potty training 34

Tips on starting potty training with your toddler 37

Signs Your Toddler Is Ready to Be Potty Trained 40

What are the signs my toddler is ready to be potty trained?
.... 41

How long does it usually take to potty train a toddler? 43

Finding the Best Potty Seat for Your Toddler 44

Choosing the best potty seat 45

A freestanding, toddler-size potty chair 45

A kid-size seat, which attaches to any full-size toilet seat 46

What to look for in a potty chair 47

What to look for in a toddler potty seat 49

Potty Training Problems 50

The difference between potty training accidents and potty training regression 51

Common causes of potty-training regression 51

Tips for handling potty training setbacks 53

When to call the doctor about potty training regression or accidents 56

How to Dress a Toddler Who's Potty Training 57

How does dressing my toddler a certain way affect her potty training success? 57

Tips on dressing your toddler who's potty training 58

Conclusions 61

Introduction

Potty training might seem like a daunting task, but if your child is truly ready, there's not much to worry about. Life goes on and one day your child will just do it. Nevertheless, most parents still have plenty of questions about ditching the diapers. One of the biggest: When should you start potty training your toddler. The answer actually varies for every child.When you have a baby, you're knee-deep in diapers. They're tucked into your bag. Stacked near the crib. Stored in boxes under beds. You might even have a few stashed in the glove compartment of your car, just in case.

Diapers are part of your life, day in, day out, for so long that it's hard to imagine not needing them anymore. It seems like the day when your child will walk into the bathroom, pee or poop, wipe, wash hands, and walk back out without you even knowing it is a long way off. And yet, that day is coming. And it'll be as glorious as it has been in your dreams. Between now and then, there's a big project: potty training, or to use the grown-up term, toilet training. You may be ready to make the transition, but is your little one. Using a potty is a new skill for your child to learn. It's best to take it slowly and go at your child's pace. Being patient with them will help them get it right, even if you sometimes feel frustrated.

Children are able to control their bladder and bowels when they're physically ready and when they want to be dry and clean. Every child is different, so it's best not to compare your child with others. Your readiness is important, too. Let your child's motivation, instead of your eagerness, lead the process. Try not to equate potty training success or difficulty with your child's intelligence or stubbornness. Also, keep in mind that accidents are inevitable and punishment has no role in the process. Plan toilet training for when you or a caregiver can devote the time and energy to be consistent on a daily basis for a few months. Does age at initiation matter? It might. A prospective study of 8000 children found that kids who started training (of any kind) after 24 months were at higher risk for experiencing slow progress and setbacks. Perhaps children who start later are more likely to resist change. But hold age constant, and your choice of toilet training methods might not matter. When a retrospective study compared child-led training and gradual, parent-led training, researchers found no differences with respect to long-term outcomes in dysfunctional voiding.

Potty Training

Whether you've reached the end of your patience changing diapers or your child wants to join an activity that requires them to be potty trained, you've decided the time has come to start potty training. Whatever life event has led you to this point, you may quickly be realizing that you don't actually know much about the specifics of potty training. (You can just tell your child to use the toilet instead of their diaper, right. In talking to people or beginning your own research on potty training, you're likely feeling overwhelmed with the differences in opinions and styles. How are you supposed to know what works best. While we can't decide for you, we are here to give you the pros, cons, and processes involved in some of the most popular potty training methods. (Also, to help you make sure that your child's really ready to potty train.

Childcare

Whether you are working full time, part time or simply need a few hours a week to yourself, sooner or later, it's likely you will need child care.

But before you start to feel anxious about leaving your child in someone else's hands, know that you're not alone. There are more than 12 million children under the age of 5 in some type of child care, and studies have shown that leaving your baby with quality caregivers can have a positive impact socially, emotionally and cognitively.

But what type of care is right for your family? From infant day care centers to nannies, there are many options for parents who need some support (and time) to work and get things done.

Making a decision is no easy task, which is why we've created this child care guide that weighs the pros, cons and costs to walk you through all the available options, along with additional resources to find care near you. The best part? Once you decide which route is best for you, you'll soon be able to rest easy knowing your little one is in caring, capable hands.

At what age can your baby start child care
If you enlist the help of a family member or decide to hire a nanny, you can begin child care whenever you're comfortable.

But when it comes to day care centers, some facilities have minimum age requirements, meaning they won't accept infants until they've reached a certain age. You'll need to make sure that the day care you're considering fits into your back-to-work timeline.

What are your child care options for an infant

Day care centers
A day care center is a state-licensed facility where parents drop off their children (mostly infants, toddlers and preschoolers) for half or full days, depending on the child care center's schedule options. These are often

large centers that group children by age in classrooms, similar to a school.

Day care pros: Day care is a great choice if you have a job with regular, fixed hours. Day care centers offer a structured day for your child, with time for outdoor play, learning, meals and naps. Socialization is a big plus. Caregivers are often referred to as "teachers" and are either working on or have completed a degree in early childhood education or a similar field. Some day care centers double as preschools, so once your child is 2 or 3, she can transition to a more formal curriculum.

Day care cons: A group environment works well for many kids, but if your child needs one-on-one attention to thrive or has special needs and requires additional supervision, day care may not be the best choice. If you think you'd have a hard time hearing your potty-trained child had an accident, or that the organic crackers you carefully packed for her snack somehow never found their way out of her little backpack, this may not be the route for you. Also, since rates are per child, the cost can be prohibitive for two (or more) children, even with a sibling discount.

How much does day care cost, Fees vary, sometimes dramatically, based on where you live. And the younger the child, the more you'll pay: By law, an infant requires a lower teacher-to-child ratio than a 4-year-old. According to a 2019 report by Child Care Aware of America, the average monthly cost of day care for an infant ranges from $480 (in Mississippi) to $1,740 (in Massachusetts). For a 4-year-old, costs range from $920 (in Mississippi) to $3,029 (in Massachusetts). Enrichment classes like music, tumbling and field trips aren't always included in the basic fee structure, so expect to pay more if you want your child to participate in those activities. And make sure you aren't late to pick up your child late fees can run as high as $1 per minute.

Family day care
Family day care, sometimes called in-home day care or home-based day care, is similar to a day care center, except it is run out of a private home with an assistant or two depending on the number of children and space.

Family day care pros: A warm, home-like environment with a smaller group of kids which results in a smaller kid-to-teacher ratio, along with the ability to mix age groups, meaning siblings will most likely stay together. Some home-based day care also is more flexible with schedules.

Family day care cons: Since there is less supervision, trust is critical — and while not always the case, caregivers may not be required to fulfill as many educational requirements as those in a day care setting.

How much does family day care cost? The cost of an in-home day care is typically less than day care centers, the national average is around $800 per month, according to the Center for American Progress.

Nanny
A nanny is a career caregiver who watches all the children in a family. For the (relatively few) parents who can provide a dedicated bedroom and bathroom, a live-in nanny is an option; otherwise, nannies are referred to as

"live out." Some nannies may do light housekeeping as part of their contract.

Nanny pros: One-on-one care by someone who will build a relationship with your child. Nannies typically want to stay with a family they like for many years, starting with newborn child care and then caring for the child as they get older, plus any subsequent siblings.

Nanny cons: You're reliant on one person. If your nanny gets a stomach bug or a flat tire, you'll need to organize backup care. Your nanny will also need to take time off throughout the year for vacations and family obligations, for which you'll also need to arrange for backup care if you don't coordinate their time off with your vacation time.

How much does a nanny cost? It depends on location, with an average hourly rate at $19.14 per hour for one child, according to the International Nanny Association's most recent pay survey that works out to $3,062 per month (if they work an average of 40 hours per week). And don't forget: When you hire a nanny, you become an employer which means that on top of their salary, you need to provide disability insurance. Plus, the IRS requires you to pay employment tax if you pay a nanny more than $2,200 per year. There are, however, several qualifiers and exceptions, so check the IRS guidelines. And because of how close families tend to get with beloved nannies, birthday and holiday gifts and annual raises or bonuses usually become part of the package as well.

Au pair
Typically, an au pair is someone from another country between 18 to 26 who comes to the U.S. on a cultural exchange via a J-1 Visa. Specialized agencies screen and train candidates and facilitate the process. Au pairs live in your house, care for your kids for a predetermined number of hours per week (no more than 45 hours), usually for a period of 12 months with the ability to extend the placement up to a maximum of another 12 months.

Au pair pros: You're getting full-time, in-home, one-on-one care for much less than what a nanny costs. This is partly because the au pairs consider being hosted in the U.S. as part of their compensation, and partly because the U.S. government sets the stipend that such workers can be paid. An au pair can be a good choice if you have several school age children with busy schedules, or if your work schedule fluctuates. You can set the au pair's schedule on a weekly basis, as long as the total number of hours doesn't exceed the agreed upon limit. Many families also love the cultural aspect: Since au pairs come from foreign countries, they bring the opportunity of immersing the kids in a new language along with stories, pictures, music and recipes from their homeland.

Au pair cons: Unlike career nannies, au pairs don't necessarily want to make child care their life's work which means they may not have the same level of enthusiasm and devotion. And while they must speak at least basic English, they might not be familiar with the U.S. let alone your town, which means there is a fairly steep learning curve. They're also not professionally trained child care workers (although they are required to have a minimum of 32 hours of child care training before they start). They can't watch infants younger than 3 months without an adult around, they need at least 200 hours of training to watch kids under the age of 2 and you can't leave your kids with an au pair for extended periods of time (say, if you go on a business trip or an adults-only vacation).

How much does an au pair cost? No less than $783 a month ($196 a week), although you can choose to pay more, but the duties and hours remain the same. The agency insures the applicants it places, so you don't need to.

Relative caregiver
A relative caregiver is a family member (mother, sister, father, aunt, etc.) who cares for your child, either at their home or yours.

Relative caregiver pros: It might seem like a dream come true to have your newborn day care provided by a relative: Who better to love and nurture your child.

Relative caregiver cons: Keep in mind that caring for a newborn is a very demanding job. Is the relative in question up to the task? Your mom might indeed be willing, but is she actually able? Older parents might not remember just how much work a baby can be. You should also consider the impact this situation could have on your relationship. For example, will you be comfortable telling your relative how you want things done? Do you think you and this relative will be able to weather any conflicts that arise? If not, it may not be worth jeopardizing your relationship by creating a potentially volatile situation. If you consider these issues and still want to proceed with relative care, be clear from the start about pay (if there is money involved), hours and duties, and be sure to have a back-up plan in place for days when your caregiver is ill or away.

How much does relative care cost? Up to you, though you may want to at least offer a weekly stipend for costs related to caring for your child.

Babysitter
A babysitter is someone who takes care of a child in your home for a short period of time and is paid by the hour. Although they often are high schoolers, college students

and even teachers looking to make extra money may also be interested in working as a babysitter. Due to their limited weekday availability, babysitters are usually used on the weekends or evenings for the occasional night out.

Babysitter pros: If all you want is someone who will keep your child happy for a few hours, a babysitter is an inexpensive solution.

Babysitter cons: Babysitters are usually not trained in any formal way and may not have enough experience to be able to properly care for young children. They tend to work out well with school age kids who are fairly self-sufficient. And because babysitters are usually on call, their availability isn't always a given.

How much does a babysitter cost? It varies based on where you live. In Denver, for example, babysitters earn under $15 an hour on average, but in New York City, you're looking at upwards of $18 per hour, according to UrbanSitter's 2020 pay survey. Sitters who are certified in CPR and first aid command more. And no matter where you live, you may be expected to pay for transportation to and from your house, as well as a higher rate for hours after midnight and holiday weekends.

Overnight nanny
Also known as a "night nanny" (not to be confused with a night nurse, who is an expert in newborn care and supports new parents in the first few weeks of a child's life), an overnight nanny is someone who stays overnight with a child often because a single parent works nights or is on a business trip. In a way, this is an easy gig for the sitter as the kid(s) will be asleep most of the time anyway unless bedtime is a challenge. In order to make this arrangement a success, establish routines and procedures in advance. And if you have a baby, knowledge of safe sleep best practices is an absolute must.

Overnight nanny pros: If you work the night shift, it's comforting to know your child is in her own bed with everything she might need or want right there.

Overnight nanny cons: If your child has a hard time settling down at night, is a restless sleeper prone to nightmares or has bedwetting issues, you might be better off with someone the child is more familiar with like a grandparent, aunt or other close relative or friend.

How much does an overnight nanny cost? Overnight sitters generally receive the same hourly rate as daytime sitters in your area.

Choosing the best child care for your baby
Where you decide to leave your baby in group day care, in-home daycare, with a nanny or with a relative comes with its own set of benefits and challenges. Narrow down which option is right for you and your family by considering the following:

- Is your schedule flexible or rigid?
- Do you often work late hours unexpectedly?
- Are you able to leave your place of work every day at the same time?
- What can you afford to pay monthly?
- How close do you want your child to be to your home or work during the day?

- And will the location of the day care be a problem if you don't go into work that day?

- Are you comfortable managing someone in your home and/or living in your home full time?

- Do you need child care every day or just a few hours a week?

If you know you want to put your baby in day care, it's never too early to start looking into group programs. That's because many facilities, especially those that accept infants, often have a long wait list especially in large cities like New York and Los Angeles.

If you want to hire a nanny or choose an in-home daycare (and even though finding a spot there isn't quite as competitive as it is for a group program), you should still start your search at least two months before you plan to head back to work.

If you're planning to leave your baby with a relative caregiver, make sure to do a couple of dry runs well in advance of your first day back on the job in case the new arrangement doesn't work out (for you or your relative) and you need to find a backup option.

Where can you find a caregiver?
Ready to start your search for your child care? For accredited day care centers, start with the National Association for the Education of Young Children (NAEYC), which maintains a list of facilities near you and is updated weekly.

You can also check out your state's government website they often have a directory of licensed child care providers, including in-home day care options, location, health and safety details, ages of children served, capacity and hours of care.

Another great way to find top notch candidates or reputable centers is word of mouth. Don't be shy about asking parents you see in your community at the playground, at Mommy-and-Me class, even at the next table at Starbucks if they can recommend a great infant caregiver.

Nursery school teachers and your child's pediatrician are also good sources, as are bulletin boards at your doctor's office, library or house of worship. And if you are looking for a nanny but want some help finding the right caregiver for your family, there are agencies that specialize in helping you find the perfect match. There is usually a fee involved, typically a percentage of the nanny's annual salary, but the nannies are vetted and a reputable agency offers a replacement guarantee. Of course, regardless of where you find your nanny, you should always call the nanny's references yourself and confirm there's been a thorough background check.

Choosing a Babysitter

At just five months, your baby likely hasn't yet displayed any of the lovely hallmarks of separation anxiety (you've still got a few months left before that delightful phase!). That's why this is a good time to spend some time away from your little darling maybe even head out for a romantic (or at least a quiet) dinner with your spouse. If you start making some baby-less forays now, parting ways and reuniting should become a little easier once the real separation or stranger anxiety actually hits.

One key to making your outings enjoyable is to feel comfortable that you've left your baby in good hands. If you've got a capable relative who's willing to step up, good for you. If not, it's sitter time! Here are some strategies on creating a safe, calm environment for yourself, your sitter, and most important, your baby.

No matter how mature your potential sitter might seem (and the younger your baby is, the older your sitter should be), make sure he or she has experience with infants, knows infant CPR, and has references (that you should definitely check!).

If possible, invite the sitter over for a visit before you actually need their services (or at least 30 minutes before you need to leave). This way the two of them can get to know each other (and you can watch the sitter in action). Some babies love everyone at first sight, so if your baby is willing to be cuddled right off the bat, great. But if your baby is shy or skittish, take it slow: Make the introduction with your baby in your arms first, then put him in an infant seat or swing near the sitter, so he can adjust to another person in the room.

Make the sitter's job easier with a quick round of show-and-tell. Show where supplies are located (diapers, first-aid kit, your stockpile of expressed breast milk or formula, the fire extinguisher, snackS). Make sure you keep important phone numbers and addresses handy, as well as leave a signed consent form authorizing certain types of medical care. Next, dish the dirty details about your baby, the best way to soothe him, his favorite toys and songs, his sleeping and eating style (he likes to be rocked, he sleeps on his side, he spits up easily, etc.) Also, don't be shy about giving instructions on how you'd like things done (e.g., how you want your baby fed, diapered, and cleaned).

Save time with future sitters by gathering this information in a binder or in The What to Expect Baby-Sitter's Handbook, which has a fill-in section you can personalize for your baby's needs (plus, it contains the essential basics of baby and child care).

Breastfeeding Your Toddler

In many parts of the world, people think nothing of seeing a tot who can walk and talk having a little nosh at his mother's breast. In this country, however, extended nursing isn't quite as common.

While some may raise an eyebrow if they spy you breastfeeding your toddler, there's a lot of official support for extended breastfeeding (which is defined as breastfeeding a toddler past age 1). The American Academy of Pediatrics (AAP) advises that continued breastfeeding has benefits for as long as mom and child want to do it. And World Health Organization (WHO) takes it a step further by recommending that babies be breastfed for 2 years or more, as long as all their nutritional needs are being met.

Benefits of extended breastfeeding
One of the benefits of extended nursing is the nutritional boost it can give a toddler, especially a picky one. In fact, experts believe that the composition of breast milk changes to adapt to a toddler's nutritional needs.

Even if your child eats like a little bird, by nursing he may make up for any deficiencies created by his pickiness. (Just don't let nursing get in the way of his meals and snacks, and continue to serve up good-for-you foods, like healthy solutions for picky eaters.)

Some other benefits of extended breastfeeding for toddlers:

1. Protection from illness. Your milk will continue to enhance your toddler's immune system so that he's less prone to colds, ear infections, allergies and other common ailments. And even if he does get sick, nursing will help to comfort him. In fact, breast milk may be the only thing he can keep down on an upset tummy.

2. A healthier future. Research has shown that breastfed babies and toddlers enjoy all sorts of health perks when they grow up, including lower blood pressure and lower cholesterol. They're also less likely to be overweight or obese, and to develop type-2 diabetes.

3. A brain boost. Though the research isn't conclusive, some studies have found that the longer and more frequently a toddler breastfeeds, the smarter he's likely to be thanks to the omega-3 fatty acids, or DHA, that are unique to breast milk.

4. Toddler independence. Rather than making him clingy, your toddler will be more comfortable exploring on his own when he knows that he always has the safety of your breast to return to.

5. Comfort. Like a pacifier or a lovey, the breast can help to calm an upset toddler or make a boo-boo feel better.

6. Quiet time. Toddlers have important work to do! They're exploring, building new skills, figuring out all sorts of things about the world. And like any worker, they sometimes need a break. Breastfeeding a toddler can provide the perfect respite during a busy day, a need that moms can certainly relate to.

Plus, there are benefits to breastfeeding a toddler for you, too. Breastfeeding can reduce the risk of certain cancers (like breast and ovarian) and help you maintain a healthy weight since breastfeeding toddlers takes energy (and burns calories).

Downsides of extended breastfeeding
Extended breastfeeding means more closeness with your child, but less time for you to take time for yourself. You may have to put off going back to work full time or committing to social or volunteer opportunities that other moms are signing up for. It may be challenging to plan when your toddler will want to nurse. Even if you were perfectly comfortable nursing your baby anytime he wanted, you may feel differently now that he's toddling around on his own two feet.

There may also be folks who criticize you for continuing to nurse your toddler, but you don't have to engage in these discussions. One way to silence them is to say that the pediatrician advised you to keep breastfeeding. A simple "doctor's orders" may suffice. Most people won't argue with instructions from a doctor.

Balancing breastfeeding with solids
Breastfeeding a toddler is a little different from nursing a baby. While most pediatric organizations recommend exclusive breastfeeding during the first 6 months, by age 1, children are getting plenty of nutrition from solid foods. In other words, there are no hard and fast rules about how much or how often a toddler should nurse or snack on solids. Most tots will call the shots.

But that doesn't mean you should give up on good manners. For the sake of your own sanity, don't feed solid foods immediately before or after a nursing session with your little one on your lap. Try to get him into a high chair and commit to a snack or small meal. Even if he rejects it by tossing it across the room, you're laying the foundation of a healthy, happy eater who may someday be welcome at a nice restaurant.

How often to breastfeed a toddler
The funny thing about breastfeeding your toddler is he's likely to tell you how often he wants to eat and when he's not in the mood for food. Even if he can't yet speak in sentences, you'll know.

Sometimes you won't want him to be quite so verbal, especially when you're out and about. So come up with a code word, phrase, or sign (maybe he can pat his chest) that will serve as a tasteful signal that he's ready for a snack. If he has a habit of grabbing at you, teach him that your shirt (and your breast) is off-limits, but he can always use the secret code word or sign to get the nip he needs.

If you're in a situation where there's no place to go when your toddler asks to nurse, make sure you have healthy snacks for kids that your munchkin can munch on until you're able to offer your breast.

Nursing positions and tips for breastfeeding your toddler
By now, your toddler is usually more interested in cruising around and exploring his world than sitting still to eat. Even if you could put him into a football or crable hold, he'd squirm out of it pretty quickly. That's fine. Most toddlers prefer to nurse sitting on your lap, with or without your arm tucked under for stability. As long as you choose a position that's comfortable for both of you, there's no right or wrong way to go.

What to do if you are criticized for breastfeeding your toddler
A short, sweet, non-defensive comeback is often the best way to handle criticism for nursing a toddler. If you've tried to put an end to the discussion on your extended nursing (and offered the "Doctor's orders" rebuttal), but someone keeps harping on it, there's nothing wrong with having a repertoire of responses to your critics. Your cousin at the family reunion says, "Is Tommy still nursing?" Just answer, "Yes," and leave it at that. In answer to, "Is he ever going to stop nursing," just say, "Yep, in about 10 minutes."

When you're ready to wean a toddler
Many nursing toddlers wean themselves. If yours won't, and you want to step up the process, try simply talking to your child.

By age 2, your child understands what you are saying. Gently let her know that the time for nursing will stop soon, but that mommy will still be there to play, read, snuggle and tickle her belly. You may want to schedule some extra fun "mommy and me" activities to soothe her fears of abandonment. It might also help to explain that graduating from nursing is something big kids do, and an occasion to celebrate.

Tips on Starting Potty Training

You may (happily) have noticed that you're changing fewer diapers lately and your little one is usually staying dry during nap time. These, along with other signs, indicate that it's time to dive into the world of potty training. The key to potty training success is patience and an awareness that all tots reach this ever important milestone at their own pace. Different strategies work with different children, but these tips generally get the job done.

How will I know my toddler is ready to be potty trained

If your little one isn't developmentally ready for potty training, even the best toilet tactics will fall short. Wait for these surefire signs that your tot is set to get started:

- You're changing fewer diapers. Until they're around 20 months old, toddlers still pee frequently, but once they can stay dry for an hour or two, it's a sign that they're developing bladder control and are becoming physically ready for potty training.

- Bowel movements become more regular. This makes it easier to pull out the potty in a pinch when it's time.

- Your little one is more vocal about going to the bathroom. When your child starts to broadcast peeing and pooping by verbalizing or showing you through his facial expressions, potty training is on the horizon.

- Your child notices (and doesn't like) dirty diapers. Your little one may suddenly decide she doesn't want to hang out in her dirty diapers because they're gross. Yay! Your child is turning her nose up at stinky diapers just like you do and is ready to use the potty instead.

How old should my toddler be when I start potty training?

Kids are generally not ready to potty train before the age of 2, and some children may wait until 3 1/2. It's important to remember not to push your child before he's ready and to be patient. And remember that all kids are different. Your child is not developmentally lagging if he's far into his 3s before he gets the hang of potty training.

Tips on preparing your toddler for potty training
She's exhibiting all the signs that potty training systems are go. But don't donate that stash of diapers just yet there's still work to do. These tips can help make a smooth transition to the active toilet-training phase:

Play up the pottying positives. Before your first diaper-free trial run, highlight the benefits of using the toilet. You might say, "Wearing underwear is fun!" or "Pretty soon you can flush, just like Mommy and Daddy!" But don't knock diapers or call your child's old habits babyish that could provoke your tot's contrarian streak and lead to real resistance.

Establish standard bathroom talk. Some experts recommend using formal words (defecate, urinate) rather than slang so kids won't be embarrassed by babyish terms when they're older but what's more important is to be consistent in your usage. And never refer to your child's diaper contents as "smelly" or "gross"; she'll be much more comfortable with toileting if she views elimination as a natural, non-"yucky" process.

Commend grown-up behavior in general. Let your child know that you support her burgeoning maturity by praising feats such as drinking from a cup without spilling and sharing toys with a friend. Don't demand too much sophistication, however if she feels pressured to perform, she may start yearning for the simpler days of babyhood (and acting accordingly).

Dress for potty training success. Get in the habit of dressing your toddler in the right potty training clothes (pants that pull up and down without any fiddling no overalls or tricky buttons), and then practice the all-important pull-down maneuver. Ask your toddler to pull down her pants before diaper changes and then pull them back up after.

Show your toddler how to use the potty. Toddlers love to mimic, and the toilet is no different. Sure, you could explain to your child how to squat, wipe and flush, but it's much more effective not to mention efficient to simply bring her to the bathroom and demonstrate. Not all parents are comfortable parting with their modesty, though, so don't feel bad about skipping this step if it's not quite your speed.

Bridge the gap between diapers and the potty. If possible, change your tot's diapers in the room where her potty is stashed this subtly reinforces the connection between the two. After she has a poopy diaper, bring her to the bathroom so she can watch you flush the contents. If she's frightened of the flushing sound, just dump and flush later.

Pick the right potty. Look for a model that's durable and won't tip over when your child jumps up to check her progress. (For an added dose of excitement, shop together for the potty and wrap it as a "gift.") Or opt for a potty seat. Some children balk at the "baby" potty and demand to use the "grown-up" one instead. In that case, buy a potty seat that simply attaches to the toilet. Look for a stable fit, a shaky seat can spook a child back into diapers for weeks and a built-in foot rest, which offers something to push against during bowel movements.

Tips on starting potty training with your toddler

Potty training is a huge milestone and for many parents a rollercoaster ride, but take solace in the fact that you've laid the groundwork and now it's time to put that potty to use.

Switch to pull-ups. When your child is just starting out on the potty, play it safe with the disposable variety. He can pull them down like underpants, but in the event of an accident they absorb like diapers and can be ripped off rather than pulled over his feet. Once your little one has enjoyed a few successes on the potty, try switching to washable cotton training pants.

Let her bare her bottom. To boost your child's awareness of her body's signals, allow her to scamper about (in a private yard or room with a washable floor) with her lower half unclad. It's hard to ignore urine when there's no diaper to hold it in. Keep the potty close by so your child can act on her body's signals quickly.

Watch closely. At this point, you might be better at detecting his body's signals than he is. Look for tell-tale signs (like fidgeting or straining) and gently ask when you suspect he has to go. Even if you're too late and he's already done the deed, have him sit on the potty anyway to reinforce the connection.

Keep her motivated. Remind her that using the potty means she's growing up. In the beginning, a small, tangible incentive can help, too for every success, try putting a sticker on the calendar or a penny in the piggy bank. As she becomes more comfortable using the potty, it's best to phase out the rewards and let her inner motivation take over.

Teach him to check for dryness. This offers him an added sense of control. If he's dry, give him a pat on the back (or a big hug), but don't criticize him if he's wet.

Be patient. Even the most enthusiastic toddler can take several weeks to master potty training proficiency often with as many steps backward as forward. If your expectations are unrealistic, you could diminish her self-confidence. Don't scold, punish or shame. No parent enjoys mopping up a puddle of pee, but try to stay cool. If you overreact, you might discourage your toddler's future attempts.

Cut the nagging. Keep it casual when reminding your tot about using the potty nagging will only provoke resistance. Similarly, don't force him to sit or stay on the potty even if you know he's about to void. (Hey, you can lead your pony to the potty, but ultimately it's his decision to use it.)

Don't deny drinks. Many parents reason that by rationing fluids, they'll cut their toddler's chances of having an accident. But this approach is unfair and unhealthy not to mention ineffective. In fact, the better tactic is to step up your child's fluid intake to give her more opportunities to succeed.

Avoid a bathroom battle. Squabbling over going to the potty is sure to prolong the struggle. If you meet with total resistance, it's best to throw in the towel (and the toilet paper!) for a few weeks. Be patient. As you wait for your child to come around, don't bring up the subject or compare him to peers who are already in underpants.

Potty training doesn't usually come easily or without bumps, so don't underestimate the process. It's all about waiting for signs of readiness in your toddler, setting the stage and diving in. While the prospect of ditching the diapers is exciting, getting there can try your parenting patience. But don't lose hope. Potty training your toddler might seem endless, but sooner or later your little one will get the hang of it and outgrow diapers.

Signs Your Toddler Is Ready to Be Potty Trained
Your neighbor boasts that her little genius was diaper-free before his second birthday. Your niece, on the other hand, refused to perch on the potty till preschool. Which is the right time frame for potty training? In a nutshell: Neither and both. As with other developmental milestones, kids are programmed with one-of-a-kind schedules and it's crucial to let your child set the pace for when to start potty training.

If your tot's not ready for potty training, even the best toilet tactics are sure to fall flat. So wait until you see these surefire signals:

What are the signs my toddler is ready to be potty trained?
1. You're changing fewer wet diapers. Until the age of about 20 months, kids pee so frequently that expecting them to control their bladders is probably unrealistic. But a toddler who stays dry for an hour or two at a stretch and occasionally awakens without wetness is physically ready for potty training.

2. Your child's bowel movements are predictable. Whether he has a BM in the morning, after meals or right before bed, a regular rhythm will help you anticipate when to pull out the potty and thus boost his likelihood of success.

3. He broadcasts bodily functions. Some children happily announce when a bowel movement is about to strike ("I pooping now!"). Others communicate through less-verbal means say, by retreating to a corner or producing a preemptive grunt. No matter what the signal, if your

child shows he's aware of his body's functions, he's ready for potty training.

4. He despises dirty diapers. At some point, most toddlers go through a (fleeting) stage when they're averse to personal messes they're bugged by errant crumbs and sticky fingers, and yes, eager to escape their soiled nappies as soon as possible. This is a golden opportunity to kick off the potty-training period because for the first time, your child dislikes his stinky diapers as much as you do.

5. He's able to perform simple undressing. When nature calls, the potty won't be of much use unless your child can quickly yank down his trousers and pull-ups or underwear. Similarly, girls should be able to hike up their skirts in a flash.

6. He understands bathroom lingo. Whether you prefer kid-friendly jargon like "poop" and "pee" or formal terminology like "defecate" and "urinate," your child's ready for potty training if he understands and is able to

use the family's words for bathroom functions and any associated body parts.

How long does it usually take to potty train a toddler?

Some toddlers pick up potty training almost immediately and for some, it takes a little longer. Your child isn't developmentally behind if he doesn't get it right off the bat or if he starts later. Some kids start around age 2 and others are well into the 3s. The process can take weeks or months, and nighttime potty training can take much longer. Most children should stay dry at night by between 5 and 7 years old. So be prepared with disposable nighttime training pants and mattress covers. For some parents, potty training can be one of the more frustrating developmental stages. Some toddlers can take longer than others and in the meantime, it can be pretty messy. But try and be patient and don't fret. Eventually your little one will learn the skill, and before you know it, you won't have to lug around your diaper bag any longer.

Finding the Best Potty Seat for Your Toddler

Potty training is an important milestone in your child's development and a welcome sign that diaper-changing may soon be a thing of the past for mom and dad. Sometime between 20 and 30 months, you'll likely notice that you're changing fewer wet diapers. That, and these other signs of potty-training readiness are your cue to pick up a toddler potty seat or chair and start potty training.

Once you do, make the new chair something your child feels comfortable with. Put it in a central place in your home (not necessarily in the bathroom at first) and allow your child to touch and observe it before using. If your child seems daunted, the American Academy of Pediatrics even recommends using imitation to show him how it's done. Here's what to consider when deciding what kind of potty-training seat, or seats, to choose for your child.

Choosing the best potty seat

For a toddler potty seat, there are two basic types to choose from, each with its own pros and cons:

A freestanding, toddler-size potty chair
Pros:

It's portable. You can take it from room to room with your toddler so it will always be close when the urge strikes. And it's so small and lightweight you can bring it on short trips (have potty, will travel!).

It's kid-size and just for your tot, which makes it less intimidating and more special than the big toilet.

It's fear-free. With no risk of falling into the water (there's no water in the bowl in a potty chair), your tot may feel more comfortable and in control. And there's no worry of your tot taking a tumble off (or into) the toilet.

Your child's legs don't dangle off this close-to-the-ground chair so she can hang out there comfortably until something happens. Plus, she'll be able to use her grounded feet to push out BM's.

Cons:

It's plastic and it's not exactly a home fashion statement. And yet something else to clutter your home with.

It's not as easy as flushing you'll have to dump out your toddler's business into the big potty (and clean the bowl)…every time.

It's not quite portable enough to take on a plane or train (how'd you like to be stopped with that in your suitcase?).

A kid-size seat, which attaches to any full-size toilet seat
Pros:

It's more like using the big toilet which can make a little one feel more like Mommy or Daddy but it's sized just right so your tot's tiny tush doesn't sink into the bowl.

It doesn't add to the clutter quotient since it sits right on top of the toilet seat.

It's totally portable it easily fits on or lifts off a toilet seat and is slim and lightweight enough to fit in your luggage. Take it along to public bathrooms on the road, on the rails, in the sky or just to a playdate. Have more than one bathroom in your house? The seat can travel from toilet to toilet.

Your toddler's pee and poop flush right down — no transfer necessary. And no cleaning out a separate bowl.

Cons:

You have to remove it when you or other family members have to use the toilet. Having people over? You'll have to remember to take the potty seat off.

It may wiggle when your tot's tush is on it, which can up the fear factor of using the big potty. For some kids, the high perch can be scary, too. And without a step stool to push against, BM's may be more of a challenge.

What to look for in a potty chair
When you're choosing a pint-size potty for your tot, consider a seat with at least some of these features, which will help make the process safer and easier for both of you.

A durable model that won't tip over when your child jumps up to check her progress.

A built-in toilet-paper holder, so your toddler has easy access to her own roll.

A compartment for books and toys, so she's got some entertainment while waiting for something to happen.

A pull-out drawer, which lets you easily dump your tot's business into the toilet and clean the potty chair's bowl.

A high back, so your child can sit and be supported comfortably

A design that gets your toddler psyched to use the chair. Take your tot shopping with you to build the excitement. Add a dose of delight by wrapping the chair and giving it as a gift. And don't forget to pick up some stickers for decoration!

A chair that comes with a removable potty seat, so you don't need to buy a toilet-seat insert once your tot is ready to transition to a big potty but still needs a more secure seat

A chair that converts into a step stool, which is handy when your tot needs a boost to get to the adult potty (otherwise you'll need a special step stool, so your toddler can safely climb onto the toilet while you supervise). Resting her feet on a step stool can also help her poop (it gives her something to push against) and feel more secure when she's high atop the adult throne.

What to look for in a toddler potty seat
When you're shopping for a potty seat, look for the following:

A dial that adjusts the potty seat to sit snugly on the toilet. The super-secure fit means the seat won't wiggle when your tot hops on important since a shaky seat can spook your child back into diapers.

If the potty seat doesn't have a dial, look for a rubbery underside, which limits slipping when your tot sits.

Handles to clutch for stability when your little one climbs on and off.

A built-in footrest, which offers a place to rest those tootsies, plus something to push against.

A removable splash guard, which may cut down on messes for little guys still perfecting their aim. If your tot finds the guard uncomfortable when he's sitting, you can just take it off and teach him to point his penis down instead when it's time to pee (it will take lots of practice).

Potty Training Problems
A few toddlers start using the potty and never look back. For most, though, accidents happen. Young kids often learn in spurts and stalls. Sometimes, they even regress, or lose skills they've recently acquired including using the toilet.

As a parent, it's natural to feel frustrated and even upset when your potty-trained child has an accident. Know that, in many cases, regression is actually a healthy emotional response to feelings your child isn't yet able to express. So your best bet to handling a potty training setback is to remain positive and take steps to help your child get back on track.

The difference between potty training accidents and potty training regression

Potty training accidents happen as your child first learns to use the toilet, it is a learning process, after all. Regression, however, is when a child who has been seemingly potty trained suddenly has accidents and/or wants to go back to wearing diapers. The good news: In most cases of regression, your child should pick right up where she left off in a few days or weeks.

Common causes of potty-training regression

Dealing with the causes of accidents is the key to putting potty training back on track, so be on the lookout for common triggers, which may include:

Lack of readiness. If the timing isn't right, even the best toilet training tactics won't prevent setbacks. Most toddlers show signs of potty training readiness between

20 and 30 months, though some will show these signs earlier or later.

Stress. Any new situation, such as a new sibling, a new sitter, a new daycare, changes to your child's regular routine or a family conflict may be stressful enough to trigger a regression in potty training.

Fatigue. Feeling tired or sluggish can prevent your toddler from reaching the potty in time to use it.

Parental pressure. Pushing a toddler who isn't ready or interested in using the toilet is likely to backfire. It's important to be patient, supportive, encouraging and reassuring during the potty training process. It's also essential to let your child set the pace.

Distraction. If your child is busy playing or engrossed in another activity, she may not notice the urge to go to the potty until it's too late, or she may choose to avoid going simply because she doesn't want to stop what she's doing.

Excitement. For tots who are new to the toilet, even just being excited can trigger an accident, they may forget to go or ignore the urge, resulting in an accident.

Inability to communicate. Your child may not have the ability to express in words any fear or anxiety she's experiencing around using the toilet or any physical discomfort she may be feeling, and it may cause her to try to avoid the potty.

Tips for handling potty training setbacks
Cleaning up puddles of pee is particularly frustrating when you thought you had already achieved this developmental milestone. But have faith that it's only a phase and your little one will move past it. These tips can help:

Be comforting. Your child may be upset after having an accident, so be sensitive. ("You had an accident, but that's okay. Lots of kids have accidents. Maybe next time you'll make it to the potty in time.") Never scold, criticize or punish your child for having a setback.

Remember the process varies for all kids. While most kids are potty trained by about 3 years old, all kids develop at different rates and some might need more time. So be sure your child is old enough and has been showing signs of readiness.

Troubleshoot. Does your child seem stressed or tired? Anxious? Talk to your child about possible triggers for the setback. ("Are you nervous about moving to our new house?" or "Has it been different with your new brother at home?") Then try to help her communicate her feelings about what's upsetting her. You can then offer reassurance to help build confidence. ("It's normal to feel scared about your new daycare. But those feelings will go away.")

Go back to potty training basics. Be clear about when and how to use the potty. Suggest regular bathroom breaks at key times, such as first thing in the morning, after meals and snacks, before a ride in the car and before bed, but try not to nag. Consider employing (or re-activating) a reward system with stickers.

Improve your child's chances for success. Keep the potty in a strategic place, and dress your child in easy-on, easy-off bottoms.

Try training pants. If you're potty training on the earlier side, training pants can make potty training less messy and help teach wetness awareness with cute graphics that fade when they get wet. If your child is potty training later, you may want to stick with pull-ups when accidents would be inconvenient (such as when you're away from home), and use cotton underwear for at-home training sessions.

Offer praise every step of the way. Help motivate your child by playing up the "big kid" angle. Focus on positive reinforcement and enthusiastic praise when she does successfully use the potty.

Give it a rest. If you've ruled out other underlying causes and your child's regression lasts longer than a month, she may simply not be ready. In that case, give potty training a break for a little while. Just get back on track as soon as your child does seem to be showing signs of readiness, since consistency is essential to success.

When to call the doctor about potty training regression or accidents

Accidents are part of the potty training process, but frequent accidents over a prolonged period could be a sign that there's an underlying medical condition that requires treatment. See your pediatrician if your toddler experiences any of these symptoms:

- Constant wetness
- Wetness following laughter
- A weak urine stream
- Painful urination or defecation
- Chronic constipation
- Blood in the urine or stool

Your pediatrician can help identify any physical or non-physical problems your toddler may be experiencing, as well as offer guidance if medications, behavior modifications or other types of treatment are necessary.

How to Dress a Toddler Who's Potty Training

The time has come to potty train your toddler. You've shopped together for a potty seat and found the perfect one. You've been reading books about potty training. Before you get started, though, you'll want to make sure your toilet-ready tot is dressed for success. Whether you have a boy or girl, your toddler will be more likely to want to test-drive the toilet if she's wearing casual clothes (no costumes or princess dresses) that are easy to take on and off.

How does dressing my toddler a certain way affect her potty training success?

What your child wears during potty training has a lot to do with how comfortable and confident she will feel practicing using the toilet, according to the American Academy of Pediatrics (AAP). General rules are to keep your child in loose, easy-to-remove clothing, and allow plenty of time to practice dressing and undressing before using the potty chair. It's a good idea to also encourage your child to sit on the potty with clothes on, then with clothes off, to make the habit seem seem less stressful.

Tips on dressing your toddler who's potty training
Follow these tips on how to dress your toddler while you're potty training her.

Ban the buttons and belts, and other fasteners she might have to fumble with. Even if she's got the dressing skills to unbuckle and unzip and manipulate other clothing closures, she shouldn't have to deal with them at the same time she's trying to get settled on the potty.

Divide and conquer. Shelve the one-piece clothing items, such as overalls, and dress your toddler in tops and bottoms. Even if that cute one-piece playsuit doesn't have difficult fasteners, it will simply take your tot too long to get it off in order to use the potty.

Be flexible. Opt for bottoms (pants, shorts) with stretchy waistbands that are easy to slide on and off. Sweatpants and leggings are ideal potty-training clothes, but you can also find little blue jeans and khakis with elastic waistbands.

Skirt the issue. At age 2 or 3, little girls are often in the dresses-only stage, so now's the perfect time to let your little princess have her way. It'll make potty training super easy, since she'll just need to deal with her underpants. Dresses can work even in winter with a pair of thick tights, as long as they're also easy to pull up and down.

Skip the shoes. Some tots like to take it all off when they go to the potty at least from the bottom down. So when you're inside, let your little one go shoeless so she can easily slide her pants all the way off when she needs to.

Keep what's underneath in mind. Underwear is a key piece of potty training clothing, so remember that what covers your toddler's cute little bum should be super comfy. Look for underpants that are 100 percent cotton and fit just right (not too tight or too loose), especially around the waist. Training pants, which have a thickly padded crotch to absorb potty accidents, are okay for some kids but others will object to extra bulk between their legs. As for colors: Obviously all-white undies will be easiest to clean after an accident (bleach to the rescue!), but allowing your child to choose from the wide array of colors, patterns and designs out there will help put a positive spin on the potty training process.

Skip the clothes altogether. Seriously. Allowing your child to run around naked, especially in the summer, can be a quick way to get the job done. Just place a potty seat in a corner of the backyard or stash a couple in strategic areas of the house so your toddler can get to it quickly when the need to pee or poop arises.

Once your child is using the potty several times a day, she may be ready to skip diapers. Disposable or non-disposable training pants can help help bridge the transition, but don't force your child out of diapers and into big kid underwear before she's ready.

Conclusions

Before picking a potty training method, it's important to take a moment to consider if your child is ready to give up their diapers. Just because you're ready to start potty training may not mean that your little one is ready, and no potty training method can change that.

If your child shows signs of regression refusing to use the toilet, withholding stools, it's important to stay calm and not punish your child. Make sure to offer your child positive reinforcement for good choices they make, and continue to encourage them to use the toilet. If frustration starts to run too high, know it's OK to take a break for a bit from potty training.

Regardless of which potty training method you choose, remember that your child will likely need a nighttime diaper long after they are daytime potty trained. Most children are capable of staying dry through the night around 4 to 5 years of age.

If you and your child are ready to begin the process of potty training, it's important to choose the right potty training method for your family. When deciding on a method, consider your child's personality, your parenting style, and the realities of your daily life.

Being potty trained won't happen overnight! It requires a great deal of patience and persistence regardless of the method you choose, but it can certainly be less stressful if you choose a method that matches your child and family.